Göbekli Tepe: The History and Mystery of One of the World's Neolithic Sites

By Charles River Editors

A picture of the excavated ruins

About Charles River Editors

Charles River Editors is a boutique digital publishing company, specializing in bringing history back to life with educational and engaging books on a wide range of topics. Keep up to date with our new and free offerings with this 5 second sign up on our weekly mailing list, and visit Our Kindle Author Page to see other recently published Kindle titles.

We make these books for you and always want to know our readers' opinions, so we encourage you to leave reviews and look forward to publishing new and exciting titles each week.

Introduction

A modern picture of the area around the site

When one thinks of the world's first cities, Sumer, Memphis, and Babylon are some of the first to come to mind, or if the focus then shifts to India, then Harappa and Mohenjo-daro will likely come up. But archaeologists recently uncovered a site thousands of years older than any of those, marking one of the oldest settled sites in the world.

One of the earliest species of the genus Homo to be discovered thus far is Homo *habilis*, which basically means "handy man." The name came from the belief at the time of its discovery that this species was the first to start using stone tools, since the first fossils to be uncovered in Olduvai Gorge were from the same stratigraphic layer as simple stone tools. Fossils of the crania and postcranial skeleton for this species have been found in both eastern and southern Africa and date to as far back as 2.5 million years ago. While other Homo species would be able to use stone tools and harness fire over time as well, the Bronze Age, marking the transition to new kinds of tools, would not come until very recently (relatively speaking).

The Neolithic period came before the Bronze Age and is generally regarded as the final subdivision of the Stone Age. During this time, communities domesticated plants and certain animals but still relied on hunting and gathering to a considerable extent, and beginning sometime around 7000 BCE, handmade pottery was developed, along with more advanced stone axes that enabled people to clear vast forests. Thanks to tools like that, the sizes of these Neolithic communities ranged from thousands to as few as a hundred, and they spread across the world with a variety of cultures and languages. One aspect these cultures had in common was that they relied on similar tools made of stone, wood, and bone.

Despite the fact some Neolithic communities grew to considerable sizes, they're typically not considered when people think of the first ancient civilizations or the first major cities, so when German archaeologists discovered the archaeological site of Göbekli Tepe in southeastern Turkey in the 1990s, it created an academic firestorm that is still raging. Far from being just another settlement, Göbekli Tepe has been described as the world's first temple and perhaps one of the locations where human civilization began. Subsequent archaeological work at Göbekli Tepe has revealed that the site was a spiritual center for the local population during a time when humans were undergoing a transition as hunter-gatherers in the Paleolithic Period to a more sedentary lifestyle in the Neolithic Period, more than 10,000 years ago. Further research in the disciplines of anthropology, religion, and history indicate that the activity at Göbekli Tepe subsequently set the tone for elements of Neolithic and Bronze Age religion and ideology in the Near East, especially in Anatolia (roughly equivalent with modern Turkey).

Although many elements of Göbekli Tepe's history remain an enigma, and probably will in the future due to the nature of the source material, the relatively recent work at the site has helped historians speculate about how Near Eastern people lived in the Mesolithic Period, how those lifestyles evolved, and how they contributed to the history of the era.

Göbekli Tepe: The History and Mystery of One of the World's Oldest Neolithic Sites

About Charles River Editors

Introduction

   The Timing

   The Modern Discovery of Göbekli Tepe

   Göbekli Tepe's Layout

   The Religious Significance of Göbekli Tepe

   The People at Göbekli Tepe

   Alternative Views

   The Decline of Göbekli Tepe and Its Lasting Legacy

   Online Resources

   Further Reading

The Timing

The lifespan of Göbekli Tepe took place during the transition from the Paleolithic to the Neolithic period, during what some scholars refer to as the Mesolithic or Middle Stone Age. The Mesolithic period was marked by shared technological and cultural features from the periods before and after it, but more closely resembled the Neolithic period, which is why experts now usually term it the "Pre-Pottery Neolithic period." About 12,000 years ago, the earliest forms of plant and animal domestication were taking place in the vicinity of Göbekli Tepe, and although there were some semi-permanent settlements in the region, people still lived primarily as hunters and gatherers.

To understand how this transition took place and the impact it had on Göbekli Tepe, it is important to go back in time a bit further. About 18,000 years ago, the last Ice Age ended, bringing warmth and longer growing seasons to much of the planet, especially the Near East (Backhenheimer 2018, 20). Although the fundamental human lifestyles did not immediately change after the glaciers receded, new and distinct cultural groups formed that would lay the foundations for such a transition.

The two earliest and most prominent cultural groups in the Near East to emerge after the Ice Age were the Kebaran, who existed from about 18,000-13,000 years ago, and the Zarzian, who were dominant from about 20,000-10,000 years ago. Both groups ranged from the Mediterranean basin to the Zagros Mountains, leaving their mark in terms of material culture for modern archaeologists to find (Bachenheimer 2018, 21). Both cultures were still hunter-gather societies, living nomadically and following their food sources, but they exhibited capabilities that would help lay the foundation for the Neolithic period.

The groups these two peoples formed were generally larger than Paleolithic groups that came before them, and perhaps most importantly, the Kebaran developed and invented bows and arrows that allowed them to hunt more game effectively. The Kebaran are also believed to have domesticated dogs (Bachenheimer 2018, 23). There is no evidence that the Kebaran or the Zarzian domesticated bovines or other animals for food sources, but a clear step forward in human development had been made.

Although the Kebaran and Zarzian provided important steps in the cultural and technological development of the Near East, they would not be the culture that ushered in the Mesolithic Era. The Natufian was the next dominant culture in the region, dominating the Mesolithic period from about 15,000-11,000 years ago (Bachenheimer 2018, 27). The Natufians inhabited much of the same territory as the Kebaran and Zarzian, and utilized the same technologies those cultures had developed, while adding their own influence by introducing semi-permanent living structures (Bachenheimer 2018, 34). It would be generous to refer to Natufian dwellings as proper houses, given that they were completely wooden and could be quickly disassembled, but the ability to live in one place over an extended period was a prerequisite for domestication. The earliest

Natufian settlements were located near game trails and edible plants, which over time led to the settlers taming the animals they once hunted and growing the plants they gathered. It is important to point out that this transition from the Paleolithic to the Neolithic Period was not uniform across the Near East - sites in lowlands generally developed quicker than those in higher elevations, while the available food sources also played a role in the size and even ideology of certain sites.

Although Göbekli Tepe was built more than 6,000 years before writing, and hundreds of years before pottery was invented, archeologists have narrowed the creation of the site to just after 10000 BCE through the use of carbon dating and stratigraphy (Bachenheimer 2018, 63). Since this period was before the invention of pottery, but after the Paleolithic period had ended, historians have termed this the Pre-Pottery Neolithic (PPN) period, which is further divided into PPN A and PPN B periods. Klaus Schmidt, who discovered Göbekli Tepe in the early 1990s and led the excavations there until his death in 2014, referred to the era as "Proto-Neolithic" and used the older term "Mesolithic" (Schmidt 2000, 48).

A picture of Schmidt

Almost as important as establishing Göbekli Tepe's chronological placement in history is understanding where it was physically located. The people who built Göbekli Tepe did so for many reasons, including proximity to resources and its spiritual setting. The first reason is relatively simple to deduce when the resources in the region are understood, but the second reason is a bit more enigmatic and continues to perplex researchers, but they tend to assume that the resources, climate, and topography of the region around Göbekli Tepe must have affected its spiritual importance.

Göbekli Tepe is in southeastern Anatolia on the edge of what is often referred to as the "Fertile Crescent." The Fertile Crescent has traditionally been defined as a wide geographical swath that encompassed the Levant and then arced to include most of Mesopotamia to form a crescent shape (Haywood 2005, 23). Although Göbekli Tepe was technically just outside the Fertile Crescent, it was also in a fertile region.

As scholars have uncovered more climate and environmental data about the Near East during the Neolithic period, it has become clear that the Fertile Crescent was just one of three fertile zones in the region. In addition to the Levant and Mesopotamia, the Zagros Mountains, which comprise Mesopotamia's natural eastern boundary and most of Anatolia, were also quite fertile. When these regions are combined, they formed a triangle – sometimes referred to as the "Golden Triangle" – with Göbekli Tepe located where all three regions converged (Bachenheimer 2018, 35). This was almost surely important in helping persuade the founders of Göbekli Tepe to choose the location, and it is also important because it no doubt helped spur later development in the region. It is important to know that the Golden Triangle region was fertile not necessarily due to its soil, although the soil was adequate for farming, but more so due to sufficient rainfall (Haywood 2005, 22). The abundant rainfall allowed hunter-gatherers to experiment with different wild crops and eventually adopt a sedentary lifestyle. Sedentary farming began in the ninth millennium BCE, and by 8000 BCE domesticated strains of wheat had been developed (Haywood 2005, 22). As noted previously, though, domestication was a long process and uneven geographically, so as some crops were eventually domesticated near Göbekli Tepe, the process happened more rapidly in other places. The location and rate of plant and animal domestication remained largely reliant upon the resources available in a particular location.

In terms of edible plants that were later domesticated, wild einkorn wheat, emmer wheat, and barley were all available near Göbekli Tepe. Wild peas, wild lentils, and wild chickpeas were also abundant in the region. Game was also quite abundant just east of Göbekli Tepe, including sheep, boars, goats, and aurochs (Bachenheimer 2018, 48). Therefore, there certainly was enough food in the area to support pilgrims who visited the site as well as a possible full-time priesthood.

There were likely other factors that played a role for the exact location of Göbekli Tepe, particularly when its relative isolation is considered. Göbekli Tepe is situated on the eastern end of the Anti-Taurus mountain ranges about seven miles northeast from the modern Turkish city of Urfa (Bachenheimer 2018, 63). Even today, the site is quite isolated and desolated: few roads lead there, and it is quite arid and devoid of most vegetation. It overlooks the Harran Plain, which is an arid steppe, but nearby is the Balikh River that comes from springs (Bachenheimer

2018, 63). It is reasonable to assume that the Balikh springs provided water for the original builders of the site as well as pilgrims and possibly priests and other residents. The site does not obviously lend itself to any spiritual significance, although its location on a hill (Turkish "tepe" and Arabic "tell") possibly points to religious significance. The site can be seen from more than 12 miles away on the plain, so it would have been a major landmark or beacon for travelers in the region (Schmidt 2000, 46). The architects of Göbekli Tepe also would have wanted to be as close to their gods as possible, so choosing a more elevated location for the temple was logical.

The Modern Discovery of Göbekli Tepe

An aerial view of the excavated areas at the site

As is the case with most major archaeological sites, the discovery and subsequent excavations at Göbekli Tepe are themselves quite a story. Few archaeologists believed there was anything worth searching for at Göbekli Tepe, so they instead focused their attention on other Neolithic sites nearby, making some incredible discoveries but allowing Göbekli Tepe to remain hidden. The discovery was serendipitous, though, because it only happened as archaeologists were working at another nearby Neolithic site.

A German archaeological team led by Harald Hauptmann began work on the PPN B site of Nevali Çori in 1982, uncovering plenty of artifacts as they continued excavations until 1992 (Bachenheimer 2018, 71). Nevali Çori is located on the Kantara River, a tributary near the headwaters of the Euphrates River (Haywood 2005, 23). Hauptmann's work at Nevali Çori was groundbreaking, as it helped historians gain insight into the transition from the Paleolithic to the Neolithic periods, particularly how the earliest sedentary communities formed throughout the Near East and the ideologies that they shared. One member of Hauptmann's team was a young archaeologist named Klaus Schmidt, who thought there was even more beneath the surface of southeastern Turkey.

Schmidt knew that there were other Neolithic sites in the region waiting to be found, but he had to narrow down potential options before he began digging. Modern archaeology is often just as political as any profession, so he needed to prove to his sponsors and the Turkish government that he was close to a discovery before he could attain funding and proper permits. To do this, he had to look to the work of Peter Benedict, an American archaeologist with the University of Chicago who had researched the area for potential archaeological sites (Bachenheimer 2018, 72). It should be pointed out that neither Benedict nor Schmidt were specifically looking for the "world's first temple," but one or more PPN sites similar to Nevali Çori. Benedict first named Göbekli Tepe as V 52/1 in his monograph of the archaeological work he did in the region from 1963-1972 with Istanbul University and the University of Chicago Research in Southeastern Anatolia program (Schmidt 2000, 45). Benedict only offered some cursory observations of the site and apparently did not think it was too important (Schmidt 2000, 46). After some diligent research of Benedict's publication and help from locals, Schmidt discovered the remains of stone tools at the summit of Göbekli Tepe, and when he could not find any signs of pottery, he knew it was a PPN site (Bachenheimer 2018, 72).

The discovery was enough to get Schmidt the permits and funding he needed to begin work at the site, and Schmidt was given the lead of a combined team from the German Archaeological Institute and the Urfa Archaeology Museum that began excavations in 1994 (Bachenheimer 2018, 73). The relatively mild climate of the region allowed for multiple expeditions per year, for a total of five by 1999 (Schmidt 2000, 46). Schmidt and his team made their most significant findings during their first few years of field work, uncovering several sanctuary enclosures, but work continues to the present. By 2012, over 43,500 square feet were uncovered, which Schmidt believed was only about 5% of the site (Bachenheimer 2019, 79). The excavations have led to a new wealth of knowledge about the PPN Near East in general and Anatolia in particular, and examining how Göbekli Tepe was built will help paint a more complete picture of this incredible archaeological site.

Göbekli Tepe's Layout

It almost goes without saying that the manner in which Göbekli Tepe was built, from the physical construction of the site to the community created it, makes it truly incredible. The builders of Göbekli Tepe had no template with which to work, so what they created was unique and inspired by the builders' imaginations. The builders' technology was also limited, and primitive by even ancient standards, and it was long believed that the kind of social structure needed to harness the required manpower for such a project was also nonexistent. Modern technology has given archaeologists some answers as to how the site was constructed, but many questions remain.

Carbon dating and stratigraphic analysis have revealed that Göbekli Tepe was built in stages, with the oldest part being built as early as 10000 BCE (Scham 2008, 23). A bit of imagination is required to reconstruct the process, but it likely began not long after the site acquired its practical and/or spiritual significance, however that occurred. Another practical reason for the location of the site was likely connected to its proximity to building materials: the limestone used was quarried nearby (Schmidt 2000, 48). This was likely the oldest stone quarry, which is obviously important, but equally important is how the workers quarried the stone and transported it to the site. The quarry workers only had stone tools at their disposal – copper tools were still thousands of years in the future – and the wheel was an early Bronze Age invention. These technological limitations meant that the workers had to use methods similar to those the Egyptians used to build their pyramids and temples. After the workers cut pieces in the quarry with their stone and wooden tools, they placed the pieces on flat boards and lifted them with ropes and pulleys and moved them across logs (Scham 2008, 26). Each of the "T shaped" pillars that are hallmarks of Göbekli Tepe are solid and weigh from two to 10 metric tons, so moving them was not an easy task and could be quite dangerous (Banning 2011, 622). Hundreds of workers were required to build the site because of the size of each pillar, the number of pillars that were used, and the danger of the work, because some workers were inevitably injured or killed and had to be replaced.

Given the mammoth scale of the project and the dangers involved, there are various questions about the nature of the site's social organization (Scham 2008, 23). If Göbekli Tepe was a religious complex as Schmidt argued and most scholars agree, then it likely would have required a priesthood. If this was the case, then the Göbekli Tepe priests may have been the first known priest class in history (Scham 2008, 26). The priesthood of Göbekli Tepe may not have been a full-time profession, which was often the case in Bronze Age societies, including Egypt, where it was for most only a part-time occupation (Shaw and Nicholson 1995, 228). Either way, questions about the division of labor and the knowledge needed to construct the site remain, because without a similar project to base the work off of, it is an open question who had the knowledge and technical know-how to construct the site, and how many workers were employed at the site.

If one looks to Bronze Age Egypt and Mesopotamia for answers, then it is likely that whatever priest class existed at Göbekli Tepe during its inception also served as engineers and technical advisors. The most educated people in Bronze Age Near Eastern societies were the priests, and priests served as their societies' scientists, doctors, and historians, so it is possible this tradition began at Göbekli Tepe. Without writing, though, these early polyglots would have had to rely on oral traditions to transmit their knowledge, which in the case of science would have been no easy task. Commanding hundreds of workers to do the difficult, dangerous manual labor required to build Göbekli Tepe would have also been difficult. The Egyptians and Mesopotamians benefited from relatively strong central governments and entrenched theological and kingship ideologies that allowed them to conscript thousands of workers at a time to build their monuments. There is no evidence that the priests of Göbekli Tepe commanded a strong central government, or that any government per se existed at the site at all, which leads to the possibility that the workers contributed to the effort of their own volition.

The number of workers required to build Göbekli Tepe and the priest class that likely worked there raise another important question: did Göbekli Tepe serve as a settlement in addition to a temple? Schmidt pointed out that there were no signs of hearths, ovens, or any other artifacts of domestic living at Göbekli Tepe, suggesting that there were little or no permanent dwellings at the site. Schmidt did concede that hunter-gathers who repeatedly visited the site for spiritual reasons could have exhausted the supply of wild game in the vicinity, so cultivation of grains and other flora may have started there at some point (Schmidt 2008, 26). An alternative view will be discussed further below, but for now it is important to consider that workers, priests, or others could have had permanent or semi-permanent dwellings nearby, just not directly at the site. The workers may also have lived in huts that simply decomposed, so evidence of their existence is gone or yet to be discovered. For the time being, although the archaeological evidence clearly demonstrates that there was considerable human activity at Göbekli Tepe, it remains undetermined if there were any permanent dwellings at the site.

Since work on Göbekli Tepe is ongoing, it is difficult to assess its true size and all its features. What has been uncovered so far though paints an image of a site that was more important than any other before it. The size alone demonstrates just how important the inhabitants of the region believed Göbekli Tepe was, and its large, relatively detailed pillars and the fact that the site was rebuilt multiple times all demonstrate that it truly occupied a central place in the world of the people of Anatolia in the Mesolithic period.

So far, archaeologists have uncovered four major enclosure sanctuaries and three minor ones. Schmidt and his team ordered the enclosure alphabetically, with Enclosure A being the first discovered and G being the most recent. The major enclosures are A, B, C, and D, and the smaller enclosures were labeled E, F, and G (Scham 2008, 23). The oval-shaped enclosures cover a 25-acre area, although as noted earlier, Schmidt believed they comprised only a fraction of the entire site (Bachenheirm 2018, 63).

A picture of the ruins of Enclosure B

A picture of the ruins of Enclosure C

A picture of the ruins of Enclosure F

Within the enclosures are pillars, which in many ways are the centerpieces and most intriguing aspects of Göbekli Tepe. Schmidt numbered the pillars in the order of their discovery, with more than 200 so far having been fully or partially excavated (Bachenheimer 2018, 77). The circular shape of the enclosures immediately led researchers to believe that they were used for ritual purposes, although the shape does not necessarily exclude a living space or a dual purpose ritual-living space. The enclosures were not uniform in size, ranging from 30 to 100 feet in diameter, with each surrounded by six-foot-high stone walls (Scham 2008, 23). A geophysical survey has indicated that there are as many as 20 more structures beneath the surface of what has been excavated, which, if they are ever uncovered, could change some of the conclusions that have already been made about the site (Scham 2008, 24). But based on what has already been excavated, it is clear that Göbekli Tepe was an important location for at least 2,000 years.

The extended period that Göbekli Tepe was in use says much about the site and the nature of religion in the Mesolithic period. The people of the region obviously thought the site was important enough to continually use it, but what is even more important is that they also built and rebuilt the site at least three times. Since the question of whether Göbekli Tepe served as a permanent or semi-permanent settlement for at least a small group of people has not been settled, scholars prefer to use the term "activity" over "settlement" when referring to the occupation levels at the site (Bachenheimer 2018, 66). There are a total of three levels of activity, with the top level being the final level of activity and bottom being the earliest, as is the case with most archaeological sites. In terms of chronology, the lop level is post-Neolithic and primarily consisted of debris, while the next level is PPN B and the bottom is PPN A (Bachenheimer 2018, 67). So far, there have been no signs of massive destruction uncovered at Göbekli Tepe, so it appears that new levels were created when structures became too old or possibly too small for the community. The archaeological evidence indicates that when the community leaders decided that a sanctuary was no longer usable, they simply filled it with material and built a new sanctuary on top of or next to the previous one (Bachenheimer 2018, 122-3).

Schmidt and his team also established that the major enclosures – A, B, C, and D – were built during the PPN A period (Banning 2011, 621). This would indicate that the PPN A was the era of Göbekli Tepe's peak prestige and likely when its nearby population would have been the highest. Therefore, it appears that construction at Göbekli Tepe began with great support from the regional population, which continued throughout the PPN A period. During the PPN B period, Göbekli Tepe's importance or relevancy began to wane, and subsequent work on the site declined.

A closer examination of this idea reveals that Göbekli Tepe was constructed in two major stages. The first stage began around 10000 BCE and ended around approximately 9000 BCE, or toward the end of the PPN A period, while the second phase ended around 8000 BCE in the PPN B period. The same architectural and artistic styles were used in both phases, but the first phase includes the most T pillars with the most intricate designs (Bachenheimer 2018, 83).

The T pillars are so named because they resemble a capital letter "T," and due to their size and location throughout the complex, they are believed to have been used as pillars. Most of the T pillars are 10-13 feet tall, with those that were likely used as central pillars a bit taller (Bachenheimer 2018, 89). Each of the pillars contains figures of animals or humans in raised relief, making them the first known examples of relief art in world history. The T pillars have no accompanying written text, so Schmidt and other experts have been forced to make educated guesses as to their meaning. Most agree that they represent how hunter-gatherers of the region viewed the world as it slowly but certainly transitioned from the Paleolithic to the Neolithic Era (Bachenheimer 2018, 90-91). At the same time, it must be remembered that these almost certainly contained religious symbolism as well.

A picture of a pillar in Enclosure B

A picture of a pillar in Enclosure C

A picture of a stone in Enclosure D

Since the T pillars in the central part of the sanctuary enclosures were a bit taller than the others, they may have had further religious significance (Bachenheimer 2018, 99). The two taller pillars in each sanctuary were in the center, perhaps acting as the centerpiece of an altar, ritual area, or other type of sacred space. The center pillars may also have had a practical use, such as holding up a wooden roof, or they could have served both purposes simultaneously. They were also unevenly distributed, at least in terms of what has been discovered so far, with Enclosure E having the fewest with two and Enclosure C having the most pillars at 19 (Bachenheimer 2018, 78).

A model reproduction of the central pillars in Enclosure D

Another architectural feature of Göbekli Tepe that remains a mystery and possibly connected to the T pillars is the monolithic stones found in some of the enclosures that have been termed "portholes." Scholars do not know what function these slabs served, but one theory is that they served as portholes. The so-called porthole stones are shaped as basins and were found scattered throughout the enclosures, so the context of their discovery has not helped scholars narrow the possibilities. The identification of the slabs as portholes or some other type of windows is certainly logical, but it raises the obvious question of why the world's first temple would need portholes or windows. If Göbekli Tepe was a religious complex, and if the enclosure sanctuaries were the most sacred areas of the complex, then a window or porthole would have little practical use. One would think that the divine would not need a window to see its worshippers, or, likewise, the worshippers need windows to see a deity or deities that manifested themselves through nature.

If the slabs were not portholes or windows, what else could they have been? An alternative explanation for the monolithic stone slabs is that they were part of a rooftop enclosure (Bachenheimer 2018, 119). Although there is no evidence that the sanctuaries at Göbekli Tepe had roofs, one theory is that they did and that the "portholes" were placed on the top-center of the sanctuaries, where they held together wooden beams that formed the skeleton of a rooftop structure (Bachenheimer 2018, 123). There is no evidence of the rooftops other than the portholes, because the skeleton was made of wooden beams and the roof was probably thatch, both of which would have degraded thousands of years ago.

A brief survey of the enclosures is also necessary to put the entire site in its proper perspective. The enclosures were the most important aspect of the site because they comprised the largest area and are the focal point of Göbekli Tepe. As interesting as the pillars may be, they were built for the enclosures, which are what made Göbekli Tepe a proper temple. Enclosure A was discovered in 1995, making it the first of the sanctuaries to be uncovered as well as the location where the fist pillar was discovered (Bachenheimer 2018, 78). The design on Pillar 1 includes five snakes and what appears to be a net of snakes, which is interesting given that snakes were not part of the hunter-gatherer diet. Pillar 2, also discovered in Enclosure A, has an image of a bull, fox, crane, and bucranium (ox head), respectively (Schmidt 2000, 49). Overall, five pillars have been attributed to Enclosure A, but there may have been 17. Enclosure A comprises 144 square feet and is a semi-rectangle with a crescent-shaped side, which is a departure from the other primarily oval and circular-shaped enclosures. Enclosure A was covered by the post-Neolithic backfill of Level III (Bachenheimer 2018, 78).

Enclosure B is slightly larger than Enclosure A at over 203 square feet and like most of the other enclosures is oval shaped (Backenheimer 2018, 78). Nine T-shaped pillars were discovered in Enclosure B, with its central pillars preserved in situ. Enclosure B's central T-pillars are quite large, at just over 18 feet, and decorated with interesting motifs (Bachenheimer 2018, 99). The two pillars have mirroring reliefs of what appear to be a fox or some type of canine (Schmidt 2000, 50). What appear to be benches run along the interior circular wall. Enclosure B was first discovered in 1998 at the same level as Enclosure A, and other than its shape, it resembles the previous enclosure in most ways. One of the more notable features of Enclosure B is its waterproof terrazzo floor (Bachenheimer 2018, 78). Although this floor predated the invention of concrete by several thousand years, the terrazzo functioned in the same way by giving the floor a hard surface above ground.

Enclosure C, which was discovered underneath the Level III debris in 1998, is perhaps the most intriguing of all the enclosures discovered so far. Positioned just to the east of Enclosure B, Enclosure C has 19 T pillars arranged in two distinct rings (Bachenheimer 2018, 89). The number of pillars and their two rings suggests that Enclosure C represented the apex of building at Göbekli Tepe, and there are other features of the enclosure that appear to corroborate this belief. The structure is comprised of two oval-shaped structures, one inside the other. The interior oval is nearly 240 square feet while the outer structure is 643 square feet (Bachenheimer 2018, 78). In addition to having the most extant pillars of any enclosure, Enclosure C's pillars also have some unique features that continue to puzzle scholars.

The T pillars in Enclosure C are notable not just for their numbers but also for the deep grooves that were cut on the top of them. 14 of the pillars at the site, in Enclosure C as well as some of the other sanctuaries, show signs of these grooves. These grooves, or notches, have provided more intellectual grist for researchers to contemplate in relation to the already enigmatic Göbekli Tepe. One of the more logical explanations for these grooves is that they served as footings for beams that were used for a roof (Bachenheimer 2018, 90-91). As with the portholes discussed earlier, this theory only makes sense if Göbekli Tepe had a roof; if it did not, then the grooves on the T pillars had to have served another purpose. Another possible explanation for the grooves may be related to how the temple was built and how the pillars were moved. The grooves could have functioned as a sort of latch for ropes that were attached to the pillars when they were pulled from the quarry, but not all the pillars had these grooves, so that theory is problematic. It also remains unknown if 14 pillars would have been enough to support roofs for all the sanctuaries, so at this point the grooves cannot be explained conclusively.

A picture of a pillar in Enclosure C depicting a fox

Another important mystery from Enclosure C is the image of a severed human head on one of the T-shaped pillars. The relief depicts a human with a severed head and a vulture standing over the scene, with a scorpion approaching from the bottom (Bachenheimer 2018, 91). At first glance, the scene appears quite chaotic and disjointed, but a comparison with other Neolithic sites from the Near East may help shed some light on its meaning. Headless corpses were discovered at the Neolithic archaeological sites in Catalhuyuk, Turkey, and Jericho, which are believed to have been part of a widespread ancestor cult in the region. Archaeologists believe that one of the essential rites of the ancestor cult was to detach and preserve the skulls of venerated relatives, likely displaying them in ritual contexts (Bachenheimer 2018, 92). The Near

Eastern "skull cult" persisted into the Bronze Age until it was replaced by the religious cults of the people who dominated the region at that time, including the Assyrians, Hittites, Canaanites, and Babylonians, but in terms of longevity, the skull cult was possibly quite older, especially if it originated when Göbekli Tepe was active. Human remains uncovered at Göbekli Tepe point toward the skull cult possibly having its origins there, or at least first being articulated in a way that survived for posterity.

The human remains discovered at Göbekli Tepe are primarily fragmentary and were not in a funerary context. With that said, most of what has been uncovered are skull fragments by a count of four to one (Bachenheimer 2018, 131). If the skull fragments discovered at Göbekli Tepe were relics of a skull cult, how would they have been displayed, and in what context? These questions are not easy to answer, but the answer to the second one would almost certainly be that these skulls were used in a funerary or religious context. The most likely explanation would be that the skulls were part of an ancestor skull cult, but they could have also been used in funerary rituals that will likely remain forgotten for eternity. How these skulls were displayed is almost as interesting and important as to why they were displayed. It appears likely that the skulls decorated the interior walls of the sanctuaries, where the priests and initiates into the skull cult would have viewed the sacred objects as they walked past the T pillars (Bacheneheimer 2018, 132). The pillars could have provided a story for priests and initiates to follow as they walked around the circular enclosures until they reached the skull wall or altar, which would have served as the center piece of the site.

A final interesting point about Enclosure C involves the relief on Pillar 12. The upper part of the relief depicts either five birds trapped in a net or wild Asiatic asses jumping over rocks (Schmidt 2000, 50). The relatively crude designs and lack of detail leave many of the designs on the pillars open to interpretation, but either possibility is interesting. If the image is birds in a net, as Schmidt argued, then it may have been an ancient snapshot of what the workmen and priests at Göbekli Tepe thought of their world as it transitioned from the Paleolithic to the Neolithic Era. The wild equines could have also been a snapshot of game in the time just before horses and donkeys were domesticated. With that said, although wild horses provided game for hunter-gatherers on the Eurasian Steppe and later became the first domesticated equines, they were not as important in Anatolia. Small, donkey-like equids were hunted in Mesolithic Anatolia, so the depiction could have been of these animals (Anthony 2007, 198).

Although Enclosure C is quite large and fairly intricate, Enclosure D – which has a similar structure comprised of a larger exterior and a smaller interior enclosure – is even larger. Enclosure D is also similar in shape as Enclosure C, with a 403-square foot oval interior and a nearly 758-square foot exterior oval (Bachenheimer 2018, 78). Located just to the north of Enclosure C, Enclosure D has 13 pillars, but the most preserved pillars and the most in one single ring of enclosing walls (Bachenheimer 2018, 90). Enclosure D was the last of the major enclosures to be discovered – in 2001 – with work on it taking place from 2002-2012

(Bachenheimer 2018, 78).

Enclosures E (nearly 299-square feet), F (304-square feet), and G (219-square feet) are all circular or oval shaped (Bachenheimer 2018, 78). In addition to having less surface area than the first four enclosures, considerably fewer pillars were discovered in enclosures E, F, and G. Only two pillars were discovered in Enclosure E, eight pillars in Enclosure F, and two pillars in Enclosure G (Bachenheimer 2018, 78). A final building, known as the "Lion Pillar Building," was discovered in 1998 and excavated during the 1998-1999 season. This structure was slightly different than the other enclosures due to several features, including its rectangular shape and smaller size, at 130-square feet (Bachenheimer 2018, 78). Only two T pillars were discovered in the Lion Pillar Building (Bachenheimer 2018, 78).

The enclosures themselves were the most important aspect of the entire site, but within them were several archaeological details that help clarify the purpose of Göbekli Tepe and who its people were. Some of these details may seem mundane at first, but a closer examination reveals they were important parts in the development of Neolithic culture in the Near East.

Enclosure C contains a set of nine limestone steps that are about eight feet long and six and a half feet high. The steps are more than 11,500 years old, which makes them the first known stairs in human history (Bachenheimer 2018, 122). The invention of stairs once again raises the issue of whether there was a permanent population at Göbekli Tepe, or not, with the creation of the stairs suggesting that the site was intended for regular use. With that said, there have been no other stairs discovered at Göbekli Tepe, so they may have been an experiment conducted by technically inclined hunter-gatherers who were simply passing through the area.

A major obstacle to Göbekli Tepe being a permanent living site, or even semi-permanent for that matter, was a lack of water. The nearest source of water to the site is about three miles to the south, which, although not extremely far, would have made sustaining a permanent population difficult. The leaders of Göbekli Tepe would have needed to marshal laborers to move water from the springs three miles away to the site every day, and if the site's population grew, it may have required multiple trips per day. Since the leaders of Göbekli Tepe likely marshalled considerable manpower to quarry the limestone and build the sanctuaries, it is possible they did the same for the water supply. Another solution could be that cisterns were used at the site. Cistern-shaped depressions were discovered next to the enclosures in the bedrock, suggesting that they were manmade formations used to hold water (Bachenheimer 2018, 124).

In addition to water, a permanent or semi-permanent population at Göbekli Tepe would have also needed a consistent food source. Animal and plant remains have been excavated at Göbekli Tepe, but they all are wild varieties (Bachenheimer 2018, 124). This does not mean that domestication of some plants and animals did not happen at or near Göbekli Tepe, only that a majority of edible flora and fauna consumed at the site was wild. It is believed that the bones of gazelles, red deer, boars, goats, sheep, oxen, and different species of birds were consumed as food and possibly as part of ritual sacrifices (Scham 2008, 26). Based on the context in which the animal and plant remains were discovered, it is difficult to determine which remains were consumed as food and which were used in rituals. If one takes the position that Göbekli Tepe had at least a small permanent population, then it is likely that a fair amount of the plant and animal remains were consumed as food. As with the later Bronze Age Near Eastern cultures, sacrificial plants and animals would not have gone to waste and would have been consumed by the priests after the rituals. The remains do not preclude small-scale domestication taking place near Göbekli Tepe, but it does not appear the site was the center of a sudden surge in domestication.

Other interesting discoveries at Göbekli Tepe include limestone heads and hundreds of lint spearpoints. Several small limestone statues and fragmentary limestone heads were discovered in the backfill that supported pillars in Enclosure D. From an art history perspective, these are among the earliest examples of three-dimensional statuary in the world, but they also help clarify Göbekli Tepe's purpose. Since art for the "sake of art" is a modern concept, archaeologists are almost certain that Göbekli Tepe's statue fragments served some type of religious or ritual purpose. One of the more intriguing theories is that there were once life-sized statues that guarded the sanctuaries, possibly standing next to or connected with the T pillars (Bachenheimer 2018, 129). It is possible that along with the skulls, they formed the centerpiece of an ancestor cult at Göbekli Tepe that later spread across the Neolithic Near East.

A picture of a boar statuette

A statuette depicting the head of an animal

A carved stone depicting an unidentified animal

The fact that hundreds of flint spearpoints were excavated among the fill layer is intriguing on several levels. Due to where they were discovered within the site, it would appear they were essentially thrown away like garbage, but that does not explain how and when they came to Göbekli Tepe. Göbekli Tepe does not have any defensive fortifications, and the site shows no signs of destruction by invaders, so it has always been assumed that the spearpoints were either brought there by pilgrims or even produced on the site. One theory is that pilgrims brought flint nodules with them to Göbekli Tepe and then fashioned them into spearpoints within the sacred precincts (Scham 2008, 26). If this theory is true, then the pilgrims may have donated a portion of the spearpoints they created as votive sacrifices and kept the rest, using them to hunt game. In this context, the deities worshipped at Göbekli Tepe would have been gods and goddesses of the hunt, much like the hunters who visited the site. Of course, like so much else, the importance and purpose of the spearpoints are still open to debate.

The Religious Significance of Göbekli Tepe

After Schmidt discovered Göbekli Tepe and initially published his theory that it was the world's first temple, most archaeologists agreed. While that is now subject to debate, it is still important to consider what ideology and theology the priests of Göbekli Tepe may have followed and how influential their religion may have been.

The theological study of the site typically begins with the important T pillars, which remain enigmatic for several reasons. First, the lack of writing accompanying the reliefs leaves scholars guessing how the images were meant to be interpreted and the context in which they were created and displayed. As was mentioned earlier, the artistic rendering of many of the figures was lacking in the style and technique of the later Bronze Age, but clearly animals comprise the vast majority of the figures and a closer look at the animals reveals some interesting details that could be connected to the theology of Göbekli Tepe.

Foxes, wild boar, and mouflon (a species of wild sheep) are more common on the pillar reliefs than gazelles and wild cattle, both of which were common among the animal bones discovered in the debris. This realization has led to speculation, with Bachenheimer suggesting that the scarcer a species at the time, the more likely it was to be represented, and that the pillars were "a transcendent summoning of their essence for the desire for greater amount" (Bachenheimer 2018, 127-8). This idea certainly sounds plausible and may be true in some of the cases, but it is also difficult to reconcile with the high frequency of snakes depicted on the pillars. There is no evidence of snake remains among the debris, so the occupants of Göbekli Tepe apparently did not eat snakes, and throughout human history snakes have been regarded mercurially at best.

Another potentially important and interesting point about the T-pillar reliefs is that "all animals are depicted as male, and no clearly female symbol is visible up to this point" (Schmidt 2000, 51). Throughout history, female deities and mythological symbols have been associated with fecundity and domestic contexts while their male counterparts were associated with warfare and the hunt. There have been exceptions to this rule – the Greek goddess Artemis was associated with the hunt and the Egyptian goddess Sekhmet was the deity of war – but this was generally the case among all cultures and all periods. The male-centric purpose of these reliefs could be related to the hunters who frequented Göbekli Tepe and possibly identified with the male game in the figures.

In addition to the natural rendering of the animals on the T pillars there was also a component of mythology present (Schmidt 2009, 47). For example, Pillar 12 depicts a band of five ducks under which is clearly a boar, and under that is a fox or another type of canine (Bachenheimer 2018, 90; 129). The fox does not appear to be hunting the ducks, nor does the boar appear hostile toward the other animals, almost creating a surreal scene where animals that would normally be hostile toward each other as predator and prey seemingly peacefully occupy the same space. This type of imagery can be viewed in other places across the world, such as in the Twentieth Dynasty (c. 1196-1069 BCE) Egyptian papyrus known as the "Satirical Papyrus." In this piece, a cat and a fox peacefully and cooperatively drive a flock of ducks (Robins 2000, 192). Although the Egyptian "Satirical Papyrus" was created in a more comedic context, it demonstrates that ancient peoples could use their imaginations to mix the natural and mythological worlds in art, which may have been the inspiration for the reliefs on the T pillars.

Another religious element of the T pillars to consider is their shape. The T shape of the pillars likely provided support, especially if there were roofs over the enclosures, but there is no practical reason why they were made in that shape. One explanation for the T shape of the pillars is that they were supposed to represent people standing with their arms out in a cross stance (Schmidt 2000, 49). This theory would certainly fit with what is known about the pillars and could work as a sort of framing device for the story told on each one. Another theological explanation for the T pillars is that the construction of them was a form of ritual and piety.

Once again, potential answers can be found in later Bronze Age Near Eastern cultures in Egypt and Mesopotamia, where the construction of temples was strongly imbued with religious overtones. Therefore, the construction of Göbekli Tepe may have been a long and ongoing ritual, indicating that the T pillars were the focal point of the religion. After the T pillars were placed in the sanctuaries, the priests would have moved past them, possibly reciting incantations as they performed their rituals. Among the most important rituals performed in many cultures throughout history are funerary rites, so an examination of the potential funerary component of Göbekli Tepe's religion is warranted.

The excavations at Göbekli Tepe have so far uncovered no tombs, although they may be beneath the enclosures that have already been uncovered (Scham 2008, 27). But even if there are no tombs on the site of Göbekli Tepe, it does not mean that the religion of the people did not articulate an afterlife or funerary rituals. It may be that the tombs of important people are located nearby but not directly on the site. Another possibility is that there were no funerary rituals carried out at Göbekli Tepe. If Göbekli Tepe was not a settlement, or only very few people lived there, then it is likely that most of the followers of the religion would have been buried in other places, following the traditions of other Mesolithic groups. It should also be noted that even later in the Bronze Age, not all cultures attributed the same importance to funerary rituals and burials. On one end of the spectrum, the Egyptians placed a paramount importance on funerary rituals and the afterlife, while on the other end of the spectrum the various cultures of Mesopotamia left very little regarding funerary rituals in their writing or material culture. The people of Göbekli Tepe may have simply followed a funerary ideology that was closer to the Mesopotamians than the Egyptians.

Based on what historians have learned from the excavations at Göbekli Tepe, a few "big picture" assertions can be made. It can be said that Göbekli Tepe was a spiritually important site to the hunter-gathers of Mesolithic Anatolia, and some educated guesses can be made as to why that was the case, but some of the details are still missing. The site was so important that was it was built and rebuilt on numerous occasions over the course of several millennia, and there was an obvious amount of skill that was involved in its creation, further attesting to the site's importance. It is now widely assumed that the site of Göbekli Tepe and the religion practiced there represented a transition from the Paleolithic to a true Neolithic religion (Scham 2008, 24). Before Göbekli Tepe, small bands of hunter-gathers practiced very personal, tribal, and localized religions, but after the site was built, there was a transition to regional religions, which ultimately paved the way for the religions of the Bronze Age (Scham 2008, 24).

However, in addition to the unknown status of burials at or near Göbekli Tepe, there are few details about the religion itself. One would presume that the people followed a polytheistic religion, as monotheism developed relatively later in world history, but it is unknown if there was an official cult at Göbekli Tepe (Schmidt 2009, 47). If one takes the stance that there was a permanent priest class at the site, then there was likely a cult with very specific rituals and ideology, but if the worshipers fulfilled priestly duties on an ad hoc basis, then the cult could have been very fluid or even nonexistent. If there was an official priest class and cult, were any or all parts of the sanctuaries off limits to non-priests? Again, because the public was only granted access to limited parts of Bronze Age Near Eastern temples, it would be tempting to think this idea originated at Göbekli Tepe, but without further evidence that can only be conjecture.

Whether festivals were held at Göbekli Tepe is another interesting, unanswered question. One could imagine festivals held to celebrate the solstices or equinoxes, but there is no archaeological evidence at the site that suggests the people recognized these events. It must also be remembered that the people of Göbekli Tepe were not yet farmers or herders, so they would not have celebrated planting or harvest.

The People at Göbekli Tepe

The background of the people who visited Göbekli Tepe and possibly lived there has been touched upon earlier, particularly the Mesolithic cultural groups to which they belonged, but it is important to examine that a bit deeper. By examining the genetics of the people of the region, along with more specific elements of their culture, it may be possible to determine if there was a permanent population at Göbekli Tepe and make an estimate on its size.

Genetic testing and DNA profiling is a relatively new technology that was introduced by British geneticist Alec Jeffreys in 1985. The initial applications of this technology were in the field of criminal justice, but it did not take long for biologists, archaeologists, and anthropologists to begin using DNA profiling on a massive scale of living humans as well as skeletal remains. DNA profiling gives archeologists another level by which they can classify people who are long gone. The first layer would be culture, which includes the languages people speak, the foods they eat, the clothes they wear, the traditions they have, the religions they follow, and other traits that bind a group together. DNA establishes the genetic ties that bind a group together, and although there is often overlap between a genetic grouping and a cultural grouping, defining the differences within a population can help scholars narrow down a particular population in a region.

Populations can be genetically subdivided into DNA haplogroups, which are populations that share many of the same genetic markers. Haplogroups can be subdivided into successively smaller groups, down to the clan or family unit. Members of the DNA haplogroup J-M304 are credited with the domestication of plants and animals in the Near East. This is a large haplogroup with many subgroups, such as J-M172, also known as "J2," which was the dominant group in the Gold Triangle region when Göbekli Tepe was built (Bachenheimer 2018, 59). These J2 people, who were later part of the agricultural revolution in the Near East, laid the genetic groundwork for the people who would build Göbekli Tepe, but just as important were the cultural traits they brought to the region. When these J2 people first came to the region of Göbekli Tepe, they were clearly hunter-gatherers, but it could be that the site's nearly 2,000 years of existence influenced their social structure as much as they left a mark on Göbekli Tepe's religious ideology. The pilgrims who visited Göbekli Tepe lived in small, egalitarian groups, which likely influenced the composition and functioning of the site, at least in its earliest phases (Schmidt 2009, 46). These early visitors of Göbekli Tepe were not members of a larger clan or an organized village but retained their small tribal structure before migrating with their game (Lichter 2007, 60). The question is, though, did this population ever become a sedentary culture at Göbekli Tepe?

While Göbekli Tepe likely had a permanent population, it was probably quite small. Specialists and builders would have had to live at the site as the new sanctuaries were being built, and it is also likely that if a priest class and official cult existed, then the priests would also have resided at Göbekli Tepe (Bachenheimer 2018, 90). But even if a relatively small population lived at Göbekli Tepe full time, then those residents would have required resources, which presents some logistical problems. The issue of water could have been solved with the potential cisterns located nears the sanctuaries – as discussed previously – but steady sources of food would have presented problems. Without the domestication of plants and animals, the priests and workers at Göbekli Tepe would have required hunters and gatherers to bring them food, which very well may have been part of the offerings. As the pilgrims brought food offerings to Göbekli Tepe, the permanent residents of the site would have allowed the visitors to manufacture flint spearpoints, perhaps leaving some as offerings. If Göbekli Tepe did have permanent residents as it appears, then it could have been the world's oldest permanent settlement in addition to being the oldest temple (Lichter 2007, 60).

Alternative Views

Klaus Schmidt's view that Göbekli Tepe was the world's first temple has been accepted by most of academia, and although he later conceded that some people could have lived at the site, he did not believe it was a true settlement. This idea has persisted in the years since Schmidt's death in 2014, with the image emerging that Göbekli Tepe was a sort of spiritual oasis in a vast desert of primitive hunter-gatherer people. Although the evidence does indicate that Göbekli Tepe was a religious site and that the human occupancy of the site is questionable, the issue is often presented in ways that ignore the complexity of the era. For example, E. B. Banning acknowledged in a study that Göbekli Tepe was likely a religious temple, but Banning also argued that the site could have housed a large human population.

Schmidt's argument that Göbekli Tepe was only a temple, with living spaces possibly nearby, was based on the theory that the people of the PPN Near East separated sacred spaces from profane spaces (Banning 2011, 619). This is not to say that the two spaces were never physically close, but that there was no overlap or dual use. Thus, while Schmidt admitted that a full-time population may have been required at Göbekli Tepe, commoners never lived in the sanctuaries that have so far been excavated. The priests and workmen may have lived near Göbekli Tepe, but there was a clear physical demarcation between their living space and where the religion was practiced. Conversely, Banning has pointed out that this was not necessarily always so clear in other places throughout the Neolithic Near East.

The lack of burials at Göbekli Tepe was discussed earlier, with the possible explanation being that they may simply be underneath the excavated sanctuaries. Banning expanded on this by arguing that in other locations in the Neolithic Near East, bodies were routinely inhumed under homes. In a number of late Neolithic Near East archaeological sites where skeletal remains have been exhumed, animal skulls and horns, as well as wall paintings, were also present, suggesting that the locations were homes and that inhumation under homes was quite common (Banning 2011, 627). The lack of human remains found so far at Göbekli Tepe could work either way in this respect. First, if no remains are found, especially if excavations are conducted beneath the sanctuaries, then Banning's hypothesis could be proven wrong. On the other hand, if remains are found, then it could be that the sanctuaries were living spaces that possibly doubled as religious spaces, proving Banning correct. The evidence is so far inconclusive, but Banning argued other elements of Göbekli Tepe strongly suggest that it was a dual-purpose site.

Banning also argued that the statues discovered at Göbekli Tepe may indicate a domestic context. Although it is generally assumed that the statues of Göbekli Tepe were made in an official capacity and probably stood in the sanctuaries, Banning noted that a human head sculpture was discovered in a house at the nearby site of Nevali Coir (Banning 2011, 628). Banning admitted that this discovery alone does not prove that the sanctuaries at Göbekli Tepe served as dual living-religious spaces, but he believed it was another piece of evidence. To bolster the finding, fragments of several others were found in other houses. This was also the case in other sites in northern Mesopotamia, not far from Göbekli Tepe, suggesting that homes could double as religious sanctuaries and vice versa (Banning 2011, 628).

As mentioned earlier, the idea that Göbekli Tepe had roofs was mentioned, but the roof's potential domestic implications were not considered. Banning noted this in his article, adding that the presence of a roof could indicate a living space (Banning 2011, 629). Banning's assertation is based on the idea that Neolithic temples were generally open spaces, such as Stonehenge or other sites discovered in the Near East, but this is not true in all cases, and because Göbekli Tepe was built so much earlier than later temples, it is problematic to assume that if it did have a roof, then it must have been used, at least partially, as a dwelling.

Banning also argued that the fill debris – namely, the animal remains – suggests that there was at least a small population that inhabited the site full time (Banning 2011, 634). Although Schmidt and other experts have not disagreed that the site was inhabited at least part time by a small number of people, they have not embraced the idea that the inhabitants lived in the sanctuaries. Banning also suggested that Göbekli Tepe could have housed a relatively large population, with there being enough game nearby to eat and water was more available at the time. Although today the area around Göbekli Tepe is arid and contains little water, Banning argued that it was more humid when the site was operating and the water table was higher, which would mean that gathering water would have been much less of a problem (Banning 2011, 635).

Banning certainly made a compelling argument for Göbekli Tepe's dual domestic-religious use, but there are two major problems with his argument. The biggest issue is that no burials have been discovered so far at Göbekli Tepe. Although some human remains have been discovered among the fill at the site, they were scattered throughout the fill, and where most of the fill was located, there were no indications the remains were part of a ritual burial site (Bachenheimer 2018, 131). It is important to point out once again that the floors of Göbekli Tepe's sanctuaries have not been excavated and Neolithic Era human inhumations in the Near East were often done underneath domestic dwellings, so it appears that this element in the debate over Göbekli Tepe's status as a religious site, settlement, or both will remain a mystery because it is unlikely excavations will go below the already uncovered sanctuaries.

Perhaps the most compelling argument made against the theory that Göbekli Tepe was a settlement is the lack of ovens, hearths, or other domestic equipment. It is a fair assumption that if the there was a permanent population at Göbekli Tepe, then there would be some archaeological signs of cooking. Banning argued that the lack of a discovery of an oven at Göbekli Tepe is not surprising, though, since almost all PPN buildings in the Near East lacked ovens (Banning 2011, 633). It should also be noted that by the very nature of the era, there would be no signs of pottery. Still, researchers think that signs of a simple hearth would have been discovered or even rudimentary utensils common in the PPN Era, such as lithic blades.

Based on the available evidence, the argument over Göbekli Tepe's permanent population remains unresolved. It is likely that a small population lived there full-time, but that the people were dependent on food from pilgrims and water was either brought in from the nearby springs or caught in small cisterns. The priests and workers likely lived in huts made of perishable materials that did not stand the test of time, while the sanctuaries were a completely sacred space. Banning offered an interesting alternative theory, but so far there is virtually no physical evidence to support his argument.

The Decline of Göbekli Tepe and Its Lasting Legacy

To place Göbekli Tepe in its proper historical and archaeological context, it is important to remember just how long ago it was built and how long it existed. From the time it was first built as early as 10000 BCE until it was abandoned around 8200 BCE, Göbekli Tepe was apparently the sole religious temple in the world. It stood as a beacon of spirituality in the emerging Neolithic Near East, but eventually it would collapse as countless temples would after it. The reasons for Göbekli Tepe's collapse are not completely understood and were likely complex, but even as Göbekli Tepe collapsed and was eventually covered by the sands of time, it managed to influence later sites throughout the Neolithic Era.

While archaeological evidence demonstrated that Göbekli Tepe was completely abandoned around 8200 BCE, how long that process took and why it happened are open to debate. The site shows no signs of sudden damage, such as burn layers, suggesting that its abandonment was gradual and not likely caused by invaders or a sudden environmental disaster. Schmidt believed that the answer to why Göbekli Tepe was abandoned can be found in the era when it existed. Göbekli Tepe was built and existed during the PPN or Mesolithic period, when humans were transitioning from a hunter-gatherer existence to a sedentary lifestyle, so Göbekli Tepe represented a religious worldview that was common among hunter-gatherers but became increasingly obsolete the more the Near East transitioned into the Neolithic Era. By the late 9th millennium BCE, domestication became more common in the region and the people saw Göbekli Tepe as an irrelevant relic of a previous era (Bachenheimer 2018, 81). As a result, the site gradually lost its prestige, fading away instead of dying out in one dramatic moment.

Nonetheless, even if the people of the Neolithic Near East may have moved on from Göbekli Tepe and its ideology, its influence reverberated throughout the region well into the Bronze Age. Just a few miles north of Göbekli Tepe near the Euphrates River, in what is today southeastern Turkey, was the equally important settlement known today by its modern name, Nevali Çori. The site of Nevali Çori has been dated to the late PPN B Period (around the mid-ninth millennium BCE), which means that the two sites existed simultaneously for a time. Unlike Göbekli Tepe, there is no debate that Nevali Çori was a settlement, but its architectural connection to the former is unmistakable. Archaeologists discovered T-shaped pillars in what are believed to have been the communal spaces of Nevali Çori, although they are smaller than those of Göbekli Tepe (Bachenheimer 2018, 88). The Nevali Çori pillars also had a similar style of reliefs carved into them, suggesting two possible explanations. Since Nevali Çori was built after Göbekli Tepe, artists and workers from the latter could have provided the knowledge and done the work on the former. The other explanation is that because Göbekli Tepe was such an important site in the region, the founders of Nevali Çori were regular visitors to Göbekli Tepe, and they brought its styles and ideas with them when they built their settlement.

Just as hunter-gatherers likely brought the architectural and possibly the spiritual ideas from Göbekli Tepe to Nevali Çori, they brought Göbekli Tepe's influence across the Near East and beyond. Atilt Yam in Israel is a notable site that resembles Göbekli Tepe, but Neolithic sites much farther away were built with the same notable stone circles. There are also notable Neolithic stone circles in Barnenez and Carnac (France), Arkaim (Russia), Nabta Playa (Sudan), and Malta. The structures at these sites were comprised of stone circles that have been described as having "transcendent meanings" throughout time (Bachenheimer 2018, 97). The similarities have led some scholars to point out that megaliths arranged in circles were common in Mesolithic England, as exemplified by Stonehenge, but none of those constructions used the T-shaped pillars (Bachenheimer 2018, 92). Thus, while it is certain that Göbekli Tepe had some influenced on Nevali Çori, how far physically that influence went, and how long it lasted, are still unclear.

In addition to the architectural influence Göbekli Tepe may have had on the Neolithic world, it also could have been one of the sources of domesticated agriculture and Neolithic Era ideology. Wheat was first domesticated just a few miles away from Göbekli Tepe, suggesting that local residents played an important role moving the region into the Neolithic period (Scham 2008, 24). Cattle were also domesticated in the Near East in the late PPN B phase, just after Göbekli Tepe was abandoned (Arbukle 2014, 281). Given those facts, Schmidt's hypothesis that Göbekli Tepe was abandoned because it lost its relevancy is more logical. As the people of the region developed and became reliant on domesticated forms of food, the hunter-gatherer religion of Göbekli Tepe no longer had relevance to them, so it was abandoned in favor of new religious views more aligned with their sedentary lifestyles.

Nonetheless, the animal figures that were so prominently displayed on the T pillars at Göbekli Tepe may have provided inspiration for later Bronze Age religions. During the Bronze Age, cattle and other domestic animals became symbols of the elite and were viewed as signs of conspicuous consumption, which may have originated in Göbekli Tepe (Arbuckle 2014, 278). Although the animals depicted and consumed at Göbekli Tepe were wild, their depictions did convey a sense of ownership, so therefore those who controlled the temple also controlled those animals, at least on the spiritual plane. The message behind the animal depictions at Göbekli Tepe may have evolved throughout the Neolithic and into the Bronze Age, but they remained symbols of power for millennia that were utilized by the elites to convey their status in society.

Online Resources

Other ancient history titles by Charles River Editors

Further Reading

Anthony, David W. 2007. *The Horse, the Wheel, and Language: How Bronze-Age Riders from the Eurasian Steppes Shaped the Modern World.* Princeton, New Jersey: Princeton University Press.

Arbuckle, Benjamin S. 2014. "The Rise of Cattle Cultures in Bronze Age Anatolia." *Journal of Eastern Mediterranean Archaeology and Heritage Studies* 2: 277-297.

Bachenheim, Avi. 2018. *Göbekli Tepe: An Introduction to the World's Oldest Temple.* Rev. ed.

Orlando, FL: Birdwood.

Banning, E. B. 2011. "So Fair a House: Göbekli Tepe and the Identification of Temples in the Pre-Pottery Neolithic of the Near East. *Current Anthropology* 52: 619-660.

Haywood, John. 2005. *The Penguin Historical Atlas of Ancient Civilizations*. London: Penguin.

Lichter, Clemens. 2007. "Vor 1200 Jahren in Anatolien." *Arcchäologie in Deutschland* 1: 60-61.

Robins, Gay. 2000. *The Art of Ancient Egypt*. Cambridge, Massachusetts: Harvard University Press.

Scham. Sandra. 2008. "The World's First Temple." *Archaeology* 61: 22-27.

Schmidt, Klaus. 2000. Göbekli Tepe, Southeastern Turkey: A Preliminary Report on the 1995-1999 Excavations." *Paléorient* 26: 45-54.

———. 2009. "Göbekli Tepe – eine apokalyptische Bilderwelt aus der Steinzeit." *Antike Welt* 40: 45-52.

Shaw, Ian and Paul Nicholson. 1995. *The Dictionary of Ancient Egypt*. New York: Harry N. Abrams.

Printed in Great Britain
by Amazon